MW00898552

PAINT THE WORLD FOR ME

BY JAMIE BULLUS

Copyright © 2021 by Jamie Bullus

All rights reserved. This book or any portion thereof may not be reproduced or used in any manner whatsoever without the express written permission of the publisher except for the use of brief quotations in a book review.

Printed in the United States of America.

ISBN 978-1-0879-4255-1

Jamie Bullus
Mount Vernon, OH, U.S.A

www.jamiebullus.com

For my world and all its colors.

With one little finger,
tap the tip of your nose.

Think of a color,
and point where it goes.

Paint the world for me,
paint it as you go.

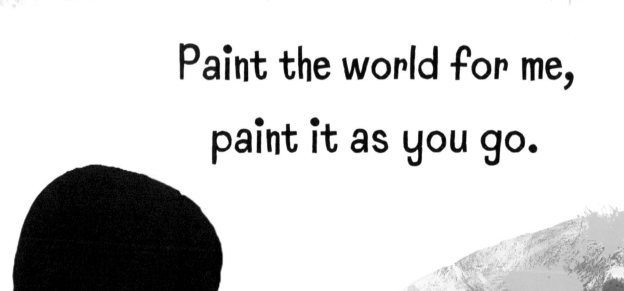

Paint it as you wish,
paint it as you know.

Paint me your mountain.

Paint me your sunrise.

Paint me your ocean.

Paint me your night sky.

What color is happy?

What color is mad?

What color is love?

What color is sad?

Paint the world for me,
paint what it could be.

Paint the dreams you dream,
paint the good you see.

Paint me your river.

Paint me your breeze.

Paint me your roots.

Paint me your tree.

What color is peace?

What color is song?

What color is laughter?

What color is strong?

Paint the world for me,
paint your highs and lows.

Paint what I don't see,
paint what I don't know.

Paint me your people.

Paint me your creatures.

Paint me your heroes.

Paint me your teachers.

What color is growth?

What color is rest?

What color is hope?

What color is mess?

Paint the world for me,
I'll paint the world for you.

Show me all your colors,
I'll show you all mine, too.

CPSIA information can be obtained
at www.ICGtesting.com
Printed in the USA
BVHW020744160621
609418BV00003B/3

* 9 781087 942551 *